T0067996

God's Cunning Women & Men

Bible Verse: Jeremiah 9:17

PASTOR MICHAEL C. CHAMPION, SR.

authorHOUSE

AuthorHouse™
1663 Liberty Drive
Bloomington, IN 47403
www.authorhouse.com
Phone: 833-262-8899

Published by AuthorHouse 03/08/2022

ISBN: 978-1-6655-5413-8 (sc)
ISBN: 978-1-6655-5417-6 (e)

Print information available on the last page.

Any people depicted in stock imagery provided by Getty Images are models, and such images are being used for illustrative purposes only. Certain stock imagery © Getty Images.

This book is printed on acid-free paper.

Cunning Expert

This book is an informational book filled with a few chapters about God's creation of all human beings. These happen to be Biblical characters who lived lives and used cunningness to their advantage. The word cunning means many things such as having skill, knowing, crafty, having skill or ingenuity, sly, skillful in deception, clever, attractive, proficient, able to be performed with skill.

Cunning is a powerful word so enjoy each chapter of this book as it deals with very cunning women and men of God.

Pastor Michael Champion

Introduction

Chapter 1

SCRIPTURE POINT: JEREMIAH - 9TH CHAPTER, VERSE 17

Thus saith the Lord of Hosts:

Consider ye and call for the mourning women that they may come and send for the cunning that they may come; quite a powerful scripture center around women, in particular Godly women.

Cunning women. The Webster New Word Dictionary defines the word cunning as having skill, knowing, clever, attractive, pretty or delicate ways, skill in deception or craftiness.

Cunning Women

My Mom who raised me- Mrs. Grace Bennett, may God rest her soul- she departed this life at 89 years old November 25th, 2020.

My first remembrance of her as a cunning woman was a story that she shared with me about my Dad who raised me, Harold Bennett, God rest his soul.

Dad was a family man, a true 'Alpha Male'. He loved his family, was a man of ethics, principles, and morals. He also dabbled in worldly things in his younger life to get ahead and support his family. He was a businessman, an earner, a hustler- whether it was owning a barbecue restaurant, shooting craps or dice, and a great pool hustler.

Mama told me the story about Daddy. He had gotten into dire straits or in a financial bind and was in real need of some loot or money. Mama said she watched seriously as he tried to beg, borrow, do everything but steal or rob to get the money needed, as he was turned down by friend after friend, relative after relative. She waited until he arrived home and asked him how much money he needed. He told her 650 dollars. She told him to come in the bedroom, as she went to the closet and pulled out several jars of his own change that she had taken out of his pockets and saved over a period of time. Needless to say it was $650 exactly. Wow. Talk about cunning women. She definitely was.

The scripture says call for the cunning women or the skilled women.

Chapter 2

EVE

I think about the first woman, Eve. She had to be cunning, don't cha think? God had given Adam the command not to eat of the Tree Of Knowledge Of Good And Evil, because God knew beforehand that not only would it cause death but it would cause the man and woman to become corrupt and become agents of Good and Evil.

Up until the eating of the fruit, they were capable of doing only good work. Talk about cunning! What trick, what deception did Eve use to get Adam, the first man, to openly before all creation to betray his maker, his God for the voice of a woman. His woman, the very woman God gave him. What did she do, what did she use?

Let's take a look. (Genesis 3:1-6)

#1- The serpent introduces himself. The scripture says he was also cunning.

#2 -And the serpent addresses the woman through dialogue or conversation. (Note) The same word in Hebrew- Serpent here in Genesis 3:1is used of literal snakes. (Gen. 3:1-14) (Gen. 49:17) (Ex. 7:15) (Proverbs 30:19)

The fact is he was a snake who walked upright. His curse was greater than any other beast proves he was a snake; a natural enemy against the man and the woman. Many people may not realize that the cunning serpent has now manipulated the woman who was a partner of Adam, a worshiper of God, a caretaker of the Garden, who has now not only listened to the cunning voice of the serpent, but now partners with him, betrays God and her counterpart Adam.

Chapter 3

What did she use on Adam to persuade him to betray his God? Satan used the serpent to deceive the woman Eve to entice Adam to join in with her betrayal of God and Adam himself.

You may not have realized it but she now has joined the serpent and developed a cunning, crafty, deceitful nature.

The serpent:

A] Questioned God
B] Misquoted scripture (Genesis 2:16-17)
C] Added to God's word

Made Eve doubt the consequences of death. He told a direct lie (John 8:44)

(First truth) at the time Adam was with Eve;1st Timothy 2:14. He should have spoke up and protected his mate.

Many of you may not understand but what has happened is the woman and man have stopped relying on God and His word and believed the lie Satan told Eve, and now have fallen from God's goodness, grace, favor.

This cunning woman enticed her husband with poison worse than arsenic. It is eternal poison and fatal, causing immediate death.

Up until this time only mankind could speak. Instead of turning away, the woman engages in dialogue or conversation with the serpent. (Don't ever listen to Satan). She did not know the serpent was her enemy.

Chapter 4

In her reply to the serpent, she leaves out the word 'all' from Genesis 2:16. She also lies and says, God said don't touch it. Eve also now being introduced to cunningness says 'Lest ye die', putting a clause to what God had definitely had declared 'Ye shall die'. Satan now has the woman's undivided attention and lies to her saying Ye shall not surely die. Wow. The woman and Adam chose to believe a lie rather than the truth. Even chooses between God and Satan by her own choice.

I pose this question again: Just what did Eve use on Adam to get him to disobey God and eat the fruit?

Chapter 5

We know it was seduction, attraction, and appeal. First seduction - mislead Adam, tempted him by holding and alluring him to eat the forbidden fruit. Adam was already awestruck with Eve's physical body. Read Genesis 2:21-23- pay special attention to Adam's description of Eve's physical body. In verse 23: bone of my bone, flesh of my flesh. In the Hebrew, Adam was really saying, Wow, what a beauty, what a body, what a beautiful human specimen. Women's physical bodies are a sight to see, that's why men usually always take a second look.

Chapter 6

Eve used enticement. She had been affected by cunningness and seduction from the serpent and now communicates the same spirit to Adam her mate. Eve took the pathway to sin and it caused the fall of all mankind.

3 steps she took:

1. She saw the tree was good for food. Sin begins with sight (Gen. 9:22), (Job 31:1). She wanted something already forbidden to her. (Sight)
2. Her desire kicked in lust, craving at all cost the forbidden fruit denounced, told not to eat, her appetite is now out of control. Desire for something wrong and dangerous, fatal. (Desire)
3. She willingly took of the fruit and ate it. (Gratification)

Chapter 7

The bad thing about sin, it usually involves others. Every sin affects someone else. In this case God and Adam, also Eve herself.

Now all humankind will be tainted by sin. There is no such thing as a private sin. Sin affects all.

Eve was attractive to Adam so it was easy for him to fall prey to her cunning ness or craftiness. Woman have a way with voice control; batting of eyelids (Isaiah 3:16}. Adam didn't stand a chance as the woman he loved turned on the charm.

She had turned on 3 fleshly fatalities:

1. The lust of the flesh, [1st John 2:15-17)
2. The lust of the eyes
3. The pride of life

Chapter 8

Cunning women are cunning by nature. Just think about it. When a woman awakes from her sleep, she has to prepare herself to be appealing. Bathe, makeup, eye makeup, sometimes lipstick, adorning of hair, nails; Men don't have to do this.

The cunningness is just natural. (Proverbs 31:26). If you would like to know the cunningness of women just talk to a man who grew up with a lot of sisters. The late entertainer, Michael Jackson, said he didn't go girl or woman crazy be cause of the negative effects that the cunningness of women had on his brothers, such as breaking valuable things, crying uncontrollably, cursing on the ground, pulling out grass- only because of the rejection or disappointment by a woman. Cunningness.

God's cunning women. After Eve and Adam fell, they became as a friend of mine, Bro. Farley. They became a strange mixture of good and evil nature, just like the tree's fruit.

Bro. Farley in his early days had been somewhat of a gigolo, using women who wanted to be used for his gain and ambition. He is now a child of the most high God.

Women are cunning and enticing, somewhat like honey- sweet. (Proverbs 5:3, 7:21) Remember in most cases a woman can always get a man to do something another man can't get him to do. Remember women always have a 'Honey-do list'. Honey do this, Honey do that.

Chapter 9

Let's look at another cunning woman from the biblical perspective [Genesis 27]. Rebekah - very cunning when it came to tricking her husband so the son could be blessed. [Genesis 27] The blessing usually would automatically go to the eldest. Now we see the cunningness and the scheming of Rebekah. It was her cunning plot that allowed her favorite, Jacob, to deceive his father out of the birthright blessing. This was done without the father's knowledge. The family had secrets and Rebekah also used the age-old special treatment of dividing children's loyalty.

It is said in Genesis 25:28, Isaac loved Esau and Rebekah loved Jacob. Since it was division in the family, there was much hatred and deception. Isaac was old and feeble. Cunning Rebekah was well aware of this and schemed to put a plan in motion to deceive Isaac through a cunning plot to get her favorite son the blessing of the family birthright. Rebekah took advantage of the situation and manipulated the circumstances to have things come out her way. What cunningness! Smart, deceptive, beautiful. Working her charm, she fulfills her well thought out plot. Jacob indeed receives the birthright and blessing and goes on to be successful.

Esau goes on also to be somewhat successful, but lives with vengeance and hatred on his mind. He was a willing participant because he sold the birthright in the first place. Now affected by Rebekah's cunning plan he seeks retribution from his brother Jacob. Rebekah uses more cunning when she further warns Jacob of his reaping from his brother's revenge to flee, run away, rather than face the wrath of Esau. In verse 45 of Chapter 27 she excuses her cunningness by telling Jacob that he did it; knowing full well she planned the trickery and scheme. She now talks about her personal pain and guilt and depression from the results of her cunning scheme. In Chapter 27, verse 45, she speaks of being weary.

Why? Because of her choices:

- Deceives husband
- Deceives both brothers
- Gets her way

Loaded with guilt, and speaks ultimately of wanting to die, because of her cunning deceitful involvement in the family's division. She never takes responsibility for her choice of actions.

Mothers: be careful that you don't cause rivalry between your family, especially children. The results will be bad.

Chapter 10

PHARAOH

The first cunning leader is a fellow by the name of Pharaoh, the name meaning 'Great House'. During the fourth dynasty (2500 B.C.) Pharaoh was a dictator, commander of armies, ruler of Egyptian people. Clever, cunning, Pharaoh loved wrong-doing.

The Pharaoh of the early Exodus had a bad taste in his mouth for Hebrews and their God, whom he didn't believe in. He was threatened by the children's fruit fullness. Chapter 1verse 10-11shows us his cunning scheme to make life miserable for God's people. Then he devised a plot to kill the Israelites newborn males. Pharaoh was intimated by the Hebrew people's growth and power. Pharaoh used all of his power to harm God's people.

In Chapter 5 of Exodus we see the cunning cruelty of the Pharaoh as he afflicts the work of the people, to make their burden of work extremely harder. Pharaoh was an agent of God, an unfair ruler, cruel. Nevertheless, God had a plan. Moses was Pharaoh's thorn in his flesh. God and Moses would deal with Pharaoh's cunning ways and craftiness. Pharaoh's cunning led to a hardened heart, stiff neck, and ultimately his demise or destruction.

His heart was hard. He was rebellious and God hardened his heart even more for God's purposes.

Chapter 11

BALAAM

This is the story of a disobedient. A prophet of God who had the power and ability to promote curses or blessings, named Balaam.

He was actually a prophet of God according to the Book of Numbers 22. What's amazing about his cunning schemes is, he was sought out by King Balak, an enemy of Israel, to curse his own people for money.

Balaam was an Edomite, a descendant of Esau. Many people think he was a soothsayer, or witch doctor, but actually he was a genuine prophet of God until he cunningly schemed to betray Israel. Question: Being a true prophet of God, why would Balaam even entertain the thought to curse Israel? It was the lure of money.

In the New Testament, 1st Timothy 6:10, warns us of the lure and power of money. Balaam was enticed by the temptation of money. To even confer with the most high God about dealing with an evil king to bring harm to God's people was not very good. But Balaam tried anyway to no avail. You see, Balaam was a cunning, skilled prophet, and he failed to realize God is the God who has stated in His word: I am the God who changes not scripture. (Malachi 3:6)

So Balaam pursues. Balaam didn't stop his involvement with the evil king. A second request was made to Balaam with even more temptation.

Balaam's first admonition - not to go with Balak. Balaam in his craftiness requests of God again to go knowing full well God is not pleased by his carnal request. After Balaam's flesh kicks in high gear and his eyes fall upon the enticing bribes Balak's messengers brought, he asks them to stay overnight; become his guests. The scripture tells us to have no fellowship with the unfruitful works of darkness. [Scripture reference Eph. 5:11]

Balaam continued to lust after money trying to figure out a way he could come out good on both ends, but it wasn't going to happen.

God answered Balaam a second time and told him to go to King Balak, but to only tell him the words that God spoke to him. But he did and didn't. This caused God to become angry at the prophet-for-hire. God sent an angel of the Lord as an adversary to the greedy prophet. If any of us become disobedient and want to sin anyway, God shows up in rebuke. Balaam got on the donkey to ride and en countered a supernatural experience. Animals always are aware of the presence more than people. Example: when the tidal wave tsunami hit Thailand people could have been saved if they just would have looked at the behavior of animals as they climbed the mountains, because they could sense danger.

Balaam's donkey didn't want to ride Balaam anywhere because he saw an angel standing with a drawn sword ready to strike and kill them. Instead of Balaam sensing this he beat the animal unmercifully until the animal talked. Yes it did. If you don't believe it, the serpent talked to Eve. Birds talk, even dogs can talk. It's true. When the animal began to talk Balaam continued to beat her even more. The donkey finally fell down and told Balaam, Why have you beat me these 3 times? Am I not the donkey you always ride, and I ride you? Can't you sense something is wrong?

When faced with pleasure and thrills we can never see clearly until it's too late. Then the Lord opened the eyes of the cunning prophet and he saw the angel with the sword ready to kill him. Then the angel said, You abused God's animal and what you are about to do is perverse. So I am sparing you only because God has a plan. When he met Balak he said, I can only speak what God has told me.

Balaam went on to bless the enemies of Balak which angered the king. Then Balaam went on to cause the children of Israel to commit sexual sin- found in Numbers 31, verse 16.

Balaam was later killed for his discretions.

Chapter 12

KING SAUL

This is information about Israel's first King. I simply call him 'The Peoples Choice'. Israel was out of order, looking for a king so they could be like the other ungodly nations around them. Saul was the peoples desire as king, not God's. So the old man Samuel, prophet-priest-judge, selected Saul to be king. God always finds His man, and when one fails Him as Saul did, He finds another. This man had many things going for him but he was also cunning, as we shall see. Physical goodness is never as good as a good character. Saul failed the test when it came to good character.

King Saul was very crafty. He had very jealous tendencies and was sort of a dictator with livid flaws in his cunningness. [Scripture 1ˢᵗ Sam. chapter 13:1]

He refused to wait for the Priest to offer up sacrifices to God and took it upon himself to step in a position he was not chosen for or anointed for and wound up being rejected by God for intruding an office he was not fit for. What could cause him to do this- power, pride or selfishness? Whatever the case this cunning decision cost him his kingship. When confronted about his mistake, he blamed the people. Saul in his cunning state was always mischievous, devious, a plotter, a schemer.

King Saul had a natural penchant for cunningness. It started with the disobedience of not following God's law to destroy King Agag and all of the spoils. It grew to jealousy, envy, rage, attempted murder upon the shepherd boy David's quest to replace him as king, per God (Jehovah's) request. Saul was a tragic figure who had been changed spiritually by God. He even prophesied he violated God's command. This led to his break with Prophet Samuel and rejection by God. The spirit of the Lord left Saul and an evil spirit replaced it, thereby releasing an even more cunning spirit.

David is sent as a musician who soothed the evil spirit. All the while, Saul's cunningness grew even more. After his proposal to the populace the anyone who defeated the giant, Goliath, would be rewarded. When he discovered it was David, he became even more jealous and envied David, thus attempting to kill David. Twenty-one attempts on his life.

His ultimate state of cunningness is when he consults the Witch of Endor. He, in his being cunning, disguises himself to approach the witch. He had her perform incantations to bring up the dead, resulting in his death and the death of his 3 sons.

He forgot the punishment for consulting a witch was punishment by God.

Chapter 13

DELILAH

There is the girlfriend of the Mighty man, Samson, named Delilah. Beautiful, crafty, cunning, she entered Samson's life while she was working the red light district.

She was a cunning harlot, or prostitute. If anyone knows the nature of a harlot, it is very cunning. Their cunningness includes her dress attire, jewelry, marks on body, makeup. [Jeremiah 4:30] She has a silver tongue. [Proverbs 2:16]

Flattering words lure men for purposes of (sometimes deadly) pleasure and money.

Harlots are known to have cold hearts, crooked minds, devious thoughts. This woman in godless, unfaithful.

Let's look at Delilah's profession. prostitute, unfaithful wife, common wife, deceiver, cunning. Samson met her while in a squabble with the enemies of God, the dreaded Philistines. He procured her sexual services and fell in love. Little did he realize her cunning spirit would be the undoing of him.

Samson being a Nazarene and also a vessel of the Almighty new full well the consequences of getting involved with an ungodly woman, but his senses, and sexuality ruled his common sense. Delilah on the other hand didn't have a Godly conscience. She was only moved by her immoral style of living and saw the man of God as a by-product to her pocketbook.

Samson lusted after her at a place called the Valley of So-rek. Notice: usually on top of things for God, he has now descended into a valley. Not a coincidence. Sin will bring you low and after meeting a woman of immoral behavior, he fell in love with her, he actually lost his first love for God and gave it to a harlot, echoing Revelation 2:4. When his enemies, the Philistines found out about his weakness for a prostitute, they immediately set a trap for his downfall. They realized Samson was no ordinary, man and possessed supernatural strength. They wanted him neutralized of his power; the same way in folklore Kryptonite rendered Superman powerless. The Philistines enticed the immoral cunning woman to betray her sensual lover Samson. So the trap was set. They enticed her with money in the New Testament. 1ˢᵗ Timothy 1:6-10 stresses the love of money is the root of all evil; causes one to stray and incur sorrows. Such was the case with the now pitiful Samson.

They offered her 5,500 pieces of silver to betray their enemy Samson into their hands. Delilah immediately set out to entice, entrap, deceive the foolish man. How cunning. Samson had become blinded by his own lust. Delilah was brutal, cunning. She used tears, charm, and pressure to get Samson to reveal his secret covenant with God which led to his downfall. Being overpowered, blinded physically, now he is in the hands and mercy of his enemies, and needs God to rescue him.

Read the story in the Book of Judges, chapter 16. Very interesting.

Chapter 14

JEZEBEL

This chapter is about one of the most cunning women who ever lived. She is talked about in both the Old Testament and New Testament of the Bible. Her name is Jezebel. This woman exhibited the spirit of a female evil, dominant, alpha woman. Cunning to the max, evil intentions, motivated by control, greed - covetous. She appears in the chapter of 1ˢᵗ Kings 16. She is the evil queen and her husband Ahab is the henpecked controlled king. They are the rulers of Israel. Ahab and his wife displayed evil always. They were Devil or Baal worshippers.

Jezebel and her wicked king of a husband practiced evil in the sight of Almighty God, Jehovah. Jezebel and an ungodly evil alliance with each other they both shunned the true living God and worshipped and built altars to worship false gods on. Jezebel true to her witch-like nature.

Ahab and Jezebel got word that a true prophet of God had arrived. They had many false prophets at their beck-and-call and had killed true prophets of God. Elijah confronts her husband and gives him a challenge to find out who the real God is in a showdown on Mt. Carmel. The true God reveals himself by fire to Elijah. In accordance with the law of God Elijah executed 450 false prophets in a zeal for the true God.

Jezebel hears about the prophet's victory and sends a death threat to Elijah who, even after seeing and knowing the awesome power of God, flees from his assignment by God. Jezebel kept up her cunning ways.

A neighbor of hers named Na-Both had a vineyard, a fertile garden. Ahab and his cunning wife wanted his property but he would not sell. So the evil Jezebel plotted to kill Naboth and steal his land. She, in royal evil cunningness took possession of his land.

Revelation 2:20 mentions Jezebel as an evil seductress. Because of her evil ways, payback is soon to come her way. The prophet exposes her evil deeds and pronounces doom on her miserable life to let her know: Be not deceived, God is not mocked. Whatsoever a man shall sow he shall reap. [Galatians 6:7] What goes around comes back around.

In 2nd Kings 9:30 Jezebel is up to her usual cunning ways and when Jehu the army commander, future king, found Jezebel she was painting her face to look good to spare her life. While hearing he was coming, she went to look out the window to see Jehu coming. He looked up and saw the evil Jezebel looking down at him and commanded the vile cunning Queen to be thrown down out of the window to the ground. So the servants threw her down and as she fell her head hit some object, her blood sprinkled, and just as the prophet Elijah had predicted in 1st Kings 21:7: the dogs did lick her blood as she lay dying, paying the full price for her cunning evil ways.

Chapter 15

KING DAVID

King David- A Hero To All of Us!

We are explicit admirers of this David fellow, called a man after God's own heart, a shepherd, warrior, worshipper of the true God. Never the less, very, very cunning.

His first act of cunningness shows when he has to face the giant Goliath to battle. King Saul tried to equip him with his armor to fight the oversized ungodly man. David quickly realized that Saul's armor did not fit him and cunningly remembered he was an expert marksman with his slingshot.

The story of this man is filled with much drama. David once a shepherd boy now on his way to become king over Israel, God's people.

Israel already had a king but it was the peoples choice of a king, God just allowed their choice. When Saul failed to meet God's standard for kingship God sent his man prophet Samuel to choose

David, a sheepboy to replace the now unfavored King Saul. David's reputation as a skilled musician and fighter helped also.

David became King Saul's companion and music player. As the relationship went on, David and King Saul's fellowship became estranged. God took his good true spirit from King Saul. Saul becomes jealous of David's favor with God and people and begins a series of assassination attempts on David's life; 21different times. It did not succeed. God protected David and David was a cunning strategist.

Saul eventually was killed and here comes the rule of King David. David becomes King, organizes his administration and fought to gain control of the land for God's people. David was labeled a hero among the people but his human side showed cunningness to be his downfall in kingship.

David should have kept his eye on God but lust first, then murder found him. He saw the man Uriah, the Hittite's, wife-nude and taking a bath upon the roof of her home and the lust of the flesh took the king over. He in his cunningness chose to take this man's wife, violate her sexually and eventually his cunningness made him think he could murder her husband and cover it up. It didn't work and caused King David grief until his last dying breath.

Chapter 16

ABSALOM

David had many children, but his son Absalom was a total thorn in David's flesh. Father and son had a love/hate relationship. Many men today deal with this problem, sometimes with their sons. Very difficult and painful. Absalom had more than being cunning going for him. He had good looks, beautiful hair and a knack for mischief.

David, his father, gave this boy unlimited favor with his father and some of this led to the malcontent between father and son. David had many children but it seems as if Absalom had a special place in David's heart.

Absalom preyed upon David's favor and many times wanted special privileges such as the time the cunning Absalom plotted to kill his brother Am-non, because of the rape he did on Absalom's sister. Even though they were brothers they were half-brothers. Same father, different mothers. Tamar, Absalom's sister, the victim of the rape was his whole sister. Absalom, filled with revenge decided to put a plan in action, [2nd Samuel], to murder his brother and avenge the honor of his sister Tamar. Absalom talked his father David into letting him and a posse of his servants to arrange some sort of celebration. This was only a ruse of plot to kill his brother.

Murder sometimes take plotting and planning, but the clever, cunning Absalom had no problem doing this. He had malice and self-justice in his heart. Remember this should have been the king's decision to take Am-non's life, not the son Absalom. But as scripture says in Proverbs 16:18, pride destroys.

Absalom had accomplished a cruel deed. Now he sets his eyes on the prize the throne of his father David. When David realized that one son had murdered the other his countenance was down. In the meantime, Absalom knew his father wouldn't approve of his misdeeds so he fled the scene. David his father was so distraught he banished Absalom from being around him. Pride began to set up in the cunning, arrogant Absalom because now he would go to the barbershop and show off his good looks and long hair for everyone to admire. Absalom started a family of his own. He thought this would mend his relationship with his father David, but nah, not so. But longing for his child, eventually David came around and allowed his cunning son to return.

Little did David the King know this was only a scheme of the cunning Absalom to devise a plan of mutiny to overthrow David's kingship. Absalom didn't think about God's proclamation in the Book of 1st Chronicles 16:22 where it declares, Touch not my anointed and do my prophets no harm. This would be the ultimate undoing of the cunning Absalom. The Bible says he requested from his father an unwarranted position to have some authority and began to steal away the hearts of the people of his father David's kingdom.

Again, Absalom had forgot God's written decree in Isaiah 54:17, No weapon formed against God's anointed will work. He went on in his cunning, prideful, bloodthirsty plot anyway. David was fully aware of his son Absalom's mutiny, but it was his child whom he loved. But as the 21st Century singing icon Tina Turner sang- What's love got to do with it? Sometime love can be misdirected or misused.

The greatest insult to his father was the cunning plot given to Absalom by David's untrustworthy adviser, Ahithophel, told Absalom to humiliate his father by taking his private women and putting them on the roof of David's house, and having sex with them all in public, in front of all of King David's people and servants. The ultimate act of betrayal

A good question would be, why would David's most important adviser supposed to be David's loyal, trusted adviser- go to a person to betray him? Remember David's great sin with the woman Bathsheba. She was Ahithophel's granddaughter. What a cunning way for payback. Why not? He hurt my family, why not hurt his. Now the destruction and downfall of the cunning Absalom.

We should remember that Absalom had a bout with vanity, because of his good looks and pretty long flowing jet black locks. This would lead to his death. After Absalom did the deeds of immorality with his father David's women, he decided to take the throne. David had to flee his throne. While chasing his father to kill him, he himself was killed when riding upon a mule, his hair was caught in the branch of the thickets allowing one of David's trusted servants to take Absalom's life.

Be not deceived, God is not mocked. Whatsoever a man soweth he shall also reap.

Chapter 17

THE HARLOT

One of the most notable people in all the ages is the harlot or prostitute. She is truly a woman of intrigue. A harlot or prostitute is a woman who mostly uses her body or sexuality for gain of money more than pleasure. Harlots or prostitutes are very clever, cunning and can be deadly. Proverbs 7 comes as a warning that all men, especially young men, to avoid her at all costs, because the price you pay for dealing with her is too steep. Prostitutes are very deceitful and have cold hearts. Don't look for love at her door, you definitely will not find it.

The harlot works just like anyone else, but her job description is pleasure and sex for sale. These women like to operate at their jobs on the street corners, especially at nighttime. Verse 7 in Proverbs says she especially likes simple men, or dumb ones. Ones who are not aware of the dangers of a prostitute. These men fall prey to their sexual urges and even mistake sexual pleasure for love and sometimes fall in love with these deadly women.

This woman is loud and stubborn, not like the Christian woman found in 1ˢᵗ Peter Chapter 3. These women are totally the opposite.

These women are vicious and seek out innocent prey just as the female lioness does on the hunt for the kill of an unwary, unsuspecting prey. These women follow suit. These women are stalkers. Bad girls as the famous singer Donna Summers said. Just listen to the words of her song, Bad girls, sad girls, out on the streets, picking up strangers for a good time, dirty bad girls.

The truth of the matter is these women have low self-esteem and morals. The result is great destruction and misery.

These women dress to seduce, wear scantily clothing, expose much of their flesh well aware that such dressing causes lust and immoral desires. These cunning women know how to bait and trap their prey: weak, lustful men whose only desire is to satisfy their flesh. Many of them committed in relationships with other women or married. They don't care. They only want to fulfill the craving of flesh-full pleasure. These women are assassins, whose job if to slay, destroy or kill unsuspecting victims such as dumb young men or old fools. The women are the crafty and cunning.

Chapter 18

THE DELIGHTFUL BLESSED
CUNNING WOMAN

The book of Proverbs 31points out a different type of cunning woman; one who pleases God and a true man desires.

The description starts out in Chapter 31verse 10, with a question: Who can find a virtuous woman, meaning she is to be sought after for her many great cunning skills. She is not ordinary, but unique, exclusive. In this case she is a married woman whose husband has total faith in her person and ability. She is faithful to him. Her husband has total trust in her as a wife.

The character this woman displays is remarkable. She has a sense of honor and respect for her husband. She always looks for the best ways to please him and satisfy his needs. This woman is not malicious or argumentative but humble, loving, wise and truly wants her husband and home to be a place of goodness.

She has no problem being the woman of the house, doing whatever chores are necessary. She cooks, cleans, washes, provides for her family. Not a complainer or whiner or rebellious, but kind, diligent. hard-working woman, mother and wife. She provides whatever is needed. She goes out of her way to make her family and household secure.

She is cunning and smart enough to shop, cook, dress her children with the appropriate clothing. She also goes beyond household duties, and shops, pays bills if necessary. She can also handle business matters if it calls for that. She wastes no energy on gossip, foolishness idle chatter or laziness. This woman is cunning and smart, wise in the greatest ways.

She looks ahead in Spring, she knows how to dress for Fall; school back in session, get the children ready. Winter - she makes sure everyone is dressed well and warm. She specializes in helping out the poor and needy. Many of these women have disappeared in the 21st Century.

As a young boy growing up in the 60's, 70's & 80's I would often see house wives and mothers with aprons on; flour & sugar on their hands & clothing, beckoning all the children to come in her house and sit at her table with her children and eat a good balanced meal. No McDonalds, no Burger King, no pizza, but a complete balanced meal such as chicken, corn, green beans, mashed potatoes, gravy, cornbread, milk, water, maybe some cold lemonade. What a shame all of these women have mostly disappeared.

The Proverbs 31Virtuous Woman is well equipped; her skills unmatched. She has such a great reputation as a cunning, wife, mother, homemaker. Her husband is well known by all people and respected.

She needs no special attention because she has earned her place. The main reason for her greatness is her love and respect for God Almighty.

What a cunning beautiful woman.

Chapter 19

THE BLESSED CUNNING MAN

Psalms chapter speaks volumes to a very cunning and smart individual. This man is smart enough, as they say, to count his chips. It says blessed is this man because he chooses his associates wisely, he chooses where he goes, he chooses God over evil. He chooses not to associate with scorners or fools. In doing so, he is blessed and cunning by his personal choices. He is smart enough to watch his ways. Proverbs chapter 16 verse 9 says a man deviseth his way or watches to his well being careful thought out choices. This man knows what he wants and where he wants to go.

The blessed man in this chapter knows where, as they say, his bread is buttered. He knows to place his affections on God first and then everything else will work out.

This man has a reverence for God's written word not only to read it but live and walk by it. He applies it to his life fully- day and night. His standing and character is sure. He knows that being in the right place at the right time with the right people only brings the best.

He knows that the will be not only successful but also safe and protected. This man prospers at whatever he chooses to do, because its right and profitable.

The blessed man in Psalms 3 is different in contrast to the ungodly men. They don't revere Almighty God, they don't make godly choices, so they are all over the place. They don't have a snowball's chance in Hell to succeed in life. Why? Because they choose not to be wise or cunning but foolish, sinful, devilish. These others choose no God and worship the creator rather than the greater.

The blessed man is exactly the opposite. He knows the way and the way of the ungodly will he not go.

Chapter 20

DANIEL: THE CUNNINGEST MAN WHO LOVED GOD

The Book of Daniel puts an awesome, faithful, Godly man on display- Daniel. Taken into captivity by the Babylonians while a young man, stood out. What made him stand out was his love and loyalty for the true and living God. Daniel is a perfect example of what dedication and faithfulness is. Daniel captured along with 3 of his friends, was described as in Daniel Chapter 4, verse 4, unblemished, favored by God, wise & cunning in knowledge and understanding science.

When put to the test of a heathens diet compared to his Hebrewish diet, Daniel purposed in his heart he would not throw away the principles and morals taught by his parents. Daniel used his cunning skills to tell the King's servant, Go Vegan. And after the 10 day test Daniel and his friends stood out in the area of countenance and health. Daniel and his friends sort of fasted or cleansed themselves by eating vegetables and drinking water. How cunning.

While in captivity Daniel was sort of forced to display his cunning skills. The King had a dream and no one could tell him the meaning. Daniel was sought out for his skills and cunningness. As Daniel began to get older his wisdom and cunningness increased. He also grew in favor and was getting famous or popular for his wisdom, skill and righteous ways of living. Note: he had been taken captive by the Babylonians and Nebuchadnezzar the King. He also was said to have outstanding, physical attraction and the ability to interpret dreams.

Throughout his life he kept his faith in God in the most difficult situations.

Daniel's faithfulness caused him to suffer at the hands of jealous, godless Babylonians who would spy on Daniel and see him pray to his God 3 times a day. They plotted against him saying he was being uncaring about the King's god and was forced to be put in a den of hungry lions. Needless to say God rescued him in his hour of trial.

Chapter 21

GOMER- BOOK OF HOSEA

The story of Gomer and Hosea is a story of unfaithfulness by a woman who was a loose woman with loose morals, very sexually active with men other than her husband, the priest Hosea. This cunning, clever woman conceived and bore a few children.

She comes into play when God commands the man of God Hosea to seek out a wife of whoredom who will bear children who you will not be the father of.

The woman Gomer with her cunning self would often forsake her husband and go after other men for the purpose of sex and pleasure, and gain money, clothes, food, drink. She just played the local whore to get paid.

This woman would run off after other lovers and her faithful husband, priest, man of God would go time and time again to bring her back home. He loved her that much.

Gomer however continued to play the whore. God allowed this cunning woman to commit unloving acts as an example to show people that just like Gomer's husband never gave up on her, God loves and never gives up on his people. He continues to rescue us no matter how unfaithful we are. Hosea, a representative of God proved his loved for God and his wife by rescuing her over and over again.

Gomer has left home to play harlot, but this time it turned out bad. She was captured by slave traders and was put on the auction block for sale. Guess who rescued this loose living woman. Why her husband, the priest, a true man of God. He saw her being sold and bought her for whatever sum of money it was and took her back home to show this cunning loose wife that his love and God's love was very real.

I think Gomer realized that her life was cruel and unjust decided to remain at home this time to raise her children and be a good wife.

Chapter 22

MEN AND WOMEN IN GENERAL

The human race is made up of men, women, boys and girls. We are very knowledgeable, capable of making things, accomplishing feats such as climbing Mt. Everest, running a marathon race, building skyscrapers, inventing all sorts of machines and gadgets.

General humankind has other skills that are far more useful, such as everyday life relationships, school, jobs, etc. These areas cause us to interact with other people and this is where cunningness plays a part.

Say a man is attracted to a young lady. How does he attract her? Good question. Many would use conversation, charm with flirting, in general flirting is a part of cunning. Flirting simply means to play at love, trifle or toy with, play at.

A good example from the biblical point of view about men and women flirting is found in the book of Genesis. Chapter 26, verse 8 mentions Isaac was sporting Rebekah, meaning to flirt with. It takes cunningness to capture a woman's heart; skill, conversation, compliments, game like a hunter captures his game, so does a man skillfully, cunningly capture the heart of the woman.

When we establish relationships, friends, businesses, games, etc., they all require cunningness. Remember the definition of cunning: skillful, clever, knowing, ingenuity, deception, slyness, crafty. All of these things come into play when humans deal with one another.

To be clever is to plot, plan a particular thing to take place, sometimes without the one it is being 'clevertized' on not to even be aware that they are a target.

We are able to craftily weave a web of lies. We are able to craftily or cunningly barter deals at rummage sales, car lots, parties, picnics, jobs, home. We are very clever or cunning at home with our families or our jobs because we spend the most time there, so we get lots of cunning practice on them.

Believe it or not, lots of cunning goes on in the church, yes the church. Remember Ananias and his wife Sapphira- cunningness proved deadly for them.

Chapter 23

THE PHARISEES

The Pharisees were Jesus' nemesis, always challenging him in every way, opposing his teaching methods and strategies. Jesus was well aware of their cunningness and dealt with them accordingly. They used much cunningness to charm the people for respect and gain. Jesus exposed them every time He had the chance. It was never his intention to humiliate or harm, but to make them aware of their wrongs.

They thrived in their cunningness to be seen of men and be praised: all opposite of what God would want out of His representatives.

They did downright cunning manipulation on the people. They demanded respect, teach people, but not practice what they preached; demanded service, not give it, seek chief places in the church, take advantage of widows, pretend to be more righteous than they were and much more; basically hypocrites.

They were very cunning at deceiving the people but they couldn't con Jesus the Christ. The Pharisees were phony, religious, very cunning. The name Pharisee means separated ones. That they did. They were the strongest religious party and opponents of Jesus' ministry and purpose.

They loved to show religious piety to the people, loved praise from human beings. More interested in impressing people than God. Putting ridiculous laws and customs on the Jewish people that they themselves didn't keep. They discredited Jesus, denying he was the Son of God. Twisted scriptures to fit them selves, not the people. With their cunning, crafty actions they misled the people. Jesus told them unless they repented, their religious actions would not get them into heaven. Some believed Jesus, only a small percentage, but the rest remained cunning and clever, denying God's real power.

Chapter 24

MALACHI'S CUNNING ISRAELITES

The Book of Malachi is a very powerful book when it comes to people giving God his true just due. Many or most of the Israelites thought they were very cunning but God knew their hearts. Malachi the Prophet wanted these cunning, selfish, disrespectful people to know and experience God's love, but their responsibility would be to honor, respect and be faithful to God -which wasn't their normal religious practiced every day way of life. But when it came down to it the people were cunning and wanted to cheat God.

This is sad because God had always been faithful to them. God had blessed them to prosper in every way and when it came to offering sacrifice to God they slapped God right in His face by giving him their worst. God had blessed them even through hardship and trial, God was always there.

These people chose to go in their barns and stables when it came to sacrifices and choose sick, blind, lame animals to offer up to God Almighty, knowing this act was contemptible, profane- they chose to do it anyway.

When God sees their treachery and cunning actions he declares they have robbed him. God lets them know he is aware of their cunning misguided actions, lets them know only if they will have a change of heart and mind he will bless them in every way. All nations shall see their change of heart and follow suit.

Only if they have a change of heart and stop their disrespect and dishonor toward Him.

Chapter 25

THE CUNNING SYROPHOENICIAN WOMAN

This particular cunning woman was very cunning. Hearing and knowing about the power of Jesus' superior abilities she sought him out to help her and her daughter.

This woman's daughter had been stricken by the possession of an unclean spirit or devil. She was totally aware of it because of her daughter's behavior; outrageous, devilish. She sought out Jesus and cunningly made a request of him to cast out the devil from her daughter. Jesus' first reaction was to refuse and test her real motive and faith.

His first comment to her was to tell her that the House of Israel was his first priority and anyone else seeking blessing was literally dogly.

She had only a limited concept of who Christ really was, her perception of him only as a healer and miracle worker was wrong. Jesus wasn't really rejecting the woman just stating a fact to her. She remained consistent and cunning in her request. How often have we remained consistent and cunning when we really wanted something really, really bad.

Jesus' reply to her did not cause her to get angry as many people would and run away, it caused her to get cunning in her thoughts. Jesus was right, she agreed, but she needed only His help. He was the only one who could change her beloved daughter. So she confessed -If I am a dog as you say, feed me, allow my request. These words stunned Christ and her granted her request.

Cunningness pays off.

Chapter 26

RICH YOUNG RULER

The Book of Luke gives us some insight on Jesus' encounter with a certain cunning rich young man. No name is given of him but the description is given about his youth, his financial status, and a view of his moral character.

Jesus had a run-in with this fellow after a brief session after teaching on parables. This young cunning fellow approached Jesus in a very cunning manner; trying to boost Jesus' ego about himself. But Jesus was very aware about his slyness.

He addressed Jesus as "good". The word 'good' was mostly related to God. It was almost never used to describe a man at that time. This man saw something in Jesus that was Good so he used the term Good Master. Cunning as he was Jesus picked up on it and asked why call me Good. The cunning fellow's response is never given but Jesus immediately responded to his request to go to heaven.

Jesus let him know that he has to be committed to righteous living in a certain way and live for God's written commandments.

After Jesus lays these things out to the cunning young rich ruler, he responds back to Jesus, I am already way ahead of you in another place. Jesus was said to have marveled at the man's response. When Jesus heard the cunning fellow want to justify his morals, Jesus quickly replied, You are on your way but some thing is missing in your life. I will tell you what it is. You are somewhat of an idolater because you possess great wealth and I am going to see what's more important to you- your stuff or your relationship with the one who is really, really good, that is God.

The cunning young man was shocked. His quest for a short trip into God's kingdom has now come to a screeching halt. Jesus makes the rubber meet the road. With this request the cunning rich young man was said to be disappointed because Jesus told him to release what was interfering with his place with God, and he was not going to do that, so he left Jesus very disappointed and sorry.

Chapter 27

A CUNNING MOTHER
MATTHEW CHAPTER 20

The story goes as Jesus was completing His ministry He was approached one day by a cunning woman who happened to be the mother of two of his main disciples, James and John, Zebedee's sons. These fellows were trusted loyal disciples working with Jesus, so I think their cunning mother figured that they had some sort of clout with Jesus and in her cunningness she would catch Jesus unaware of her scheme.

Jesus was always alert and sharp. This mother was a very loving mother because she wanted to secure her sons' permanent status. Her request was both cunning and bold. She was a true mom at best. Jesus let her know she was making a request that has an awesome price tag associated with it - suffering, persecution at the least. But the boys were also eager to see the cunning scheme work by saying we can handle anything that comes our way. Jesus lets them know: You are going to receive a lot of adverse drama by just being associated with me, but the request your mother is requesting is not in my power to grant.

Now the other 10 Disciples were very aware of the cunning mother's request for her sons' promotion over the other disciples.

This caused problems for the infrastructure of the group. So much so that they were very angry with the two brothers. Jesus quickly put all of them in their place - a place of humility. This cunning mother's request was denied.

Chapter 28

THE CUNNING RICH MAN LUKE 12

Jesus was approached by two brothers who had a dispute over money and property, so Jesus told them a story of a very cunning rich man who had prospered greatly.

His finances came mostly from farming and agriculture. He was very rich.

In his cunning head he realized that he had it going on and thought it okay to be greedy and suggested to his cunning self: I am going to stock up my goods and live it up.

His motivation was total selfishness. He was in a position to help aid and assist many people but in his cunningness he only thought of himself. Even suggesting to himself, not anticipating anything could go wrong. I'm gonna live it up, all by myself

He even talked about being in total control of his soul, forgetting God said in His word All souls are mine. He thought in his craftiness that he was going to experience longevity in his life so he told the illusion that everything past, present and future would be all good.

Little did he in his clever self not know that God is in control. While he was in his delusional state, God appeared to this cunning, cool, as the Bible calls him A Foolish Man, and let him know that death was immediately imminent, and he was about to die and everything he chose to enjoy was going to someone else.

How sad this cunning man's life ended.

Chapter 29

ZACCHAEUS

This story starts out with a very desperate rich man who had cunningly became rich. Even though he was rich in money and material goods it is quite obvious in all of his cunning efforts something was lacking.

He had heard the stories about Jesus' ability to heal, set free, save and deliver and he desired that. In his desperation he realized it would be very hard to get to Jesus physically, because Jesus had become popular, in demand and much wanted by many, many people. In all of his person Zacchaeus was short in stature, big in success. But lacking in height and knew it would be almost impossible to get to Jesus, after all, Zacchaeus was not about to grow anymore.

So he became clever or cunning, and had mapped out Jesus' route in his desperate desire to see Jesus. He saw a large sycamore tree and said, I know how to get Jesus' attention. I will climb that tree. So he climbed up the tree. Because of his height it was very   possible he felt inferior in his stature. He wanted to see Jesus so badly he forgot about his status and worth and humbled himself enough to climb that tree to see Jesus.

Jesus passing by looked up and saw the desperate sinner, gave him the invitation to come down and join. He complied, got saved and it changed his life entirely.

Chapter 30

SIMON PETER

Jesus was introduced to the cunning and bold Simon Peter through his brother Andrew. Upon meeting Jesus (John 1:40} tells us of the intro. Andrew tells his brother: "We have found the Messiah" when introducing Andrew to Jesus. Jesus immediately recognized the hardness and cunningness of Peter and addressed him a cephas, meaning a stone, hard one. Peter became an instant follower of Jesus. Many times in his cunningness he would speak out of turn, or even challenge Jesus at times. Jesus was to Peter what water was to a fish. Jesus was his lifeline.

His cunningness shows up very often. For example, realizing that Jesus was the only true lifeline to heaven in John chapter 6, verse 68. Jesus had preached one awesome sermon to the crowd and many of them were offended and walked away, but Peter in his cunningness knew that Christ was the only answer, declaring his total loyalty to Christ.

On another occasion in Matthew 16:16, Peter had a revelation who Christ really was: The Messiah, not a man, the Son of God, sent by God, to fulfill all the prophets had said. This display of cunningness by Peter was not his own but God's, who had a special place for the impetuous.

Peter was convinced in himself but awakened by the spiritual revelation from God the Father, who wanted to reveal to him only at that time that Jesus was the true sent one from God to save the world.

Peter's cunningness paid off.

Chapter 31

JUDAS ISCARIOT

This is the only revelation of God that Judas lscariot is in; the last chapter of this book about cunning women & men.

I think Judas was the most cunning and dangerous of all mankind. After alt he was a disciple of Jesus but aptly called a devil by Jesus himself in John chapter 6. Cunning, devilish, selfish thief - this describes Judas. A follower of Christ, always scheming; Judas was a hater.

Jesus was well aware of Judas' cunning, clever actions but he needed Judas to fulfill his mission. Judas a devil, a betrayer, a thief, was always plotting just like the woman who anointed Jesus' feet in honor of what Jesus did for her. Judas spoke up about the woman's gift like he really cared. He only wanted her to give the perfume to Jesus. It was very expensive and Judas said in his cunningness that it could have been sold to give the money to the poor, like he cared.

He was the thief of all the disciples. Judas became angry, envious, and disappointed at Jesus and plotted a cunning move with Jesus' enemies to betray him at The last Supper. Judas' cunningness went to another level. Jesus was well aware of his cunning deception and co-signed the plot of Judas.

This would be the last straw for the cunning devilish Judas. It claimed his own life.

Printed in the United States
by Baker & Taylor Publisher Services